THE WONDER OF WOLVES

A Story & Activities

Sandra Chisholm Robinson, author

Gail Kohler Opsahl, illustrator

Published by

Denver Museum of Natural History

In Cooperation with

Roberts Rinehart, Inc. Publishers

CONTENTS

O THE PARENT

The story, mask and activities in this book are to be shared and enjoyed by you and your child. We recommend that you read the story together first and then proceed with the activities. Although you may do the activities in any order, they have been designed so that the information grows in a logical fashion from one game or puzzle to the next. We hope that this book will be just the beginning of your exploration of the wonder of wolves!

Copyright ©1989 by the Denver Museum of Natural History
Published by Roberts Rinehart, Inc. Publishers
Post Office Box 3161, Boulder, Colorado 80303
International Standard Book Number 0-911797-65-3
Manufactured in the United States of America

The following story tells of a special bond between people and wolves. The people are the Nuu-chah-nulth, the West Coast People (formerly known as the Nootka Indians). They lived on the west coast of Vancouver Island. (SEE MAP) This island is part of British Columbia, which is a province (like a state) of Canada.

CANADA

VANCOUVER ISLAND

PACIFIC OCEAN

WASHINGTON STATE

Although this story is fiction (written from the author's imagination), a portion of it was suggested from the child-hood of a living North American Indian, Art Thompson.

Art Thompson is a west coast Canadian artist who continues the traditions of the Nuu-chah-nulth by singing family songs, learning the old stories, carving beautiful masks, and leading a wolf ceremonial dance.

The west coast people thought of the wolf as a friend . . . a brother. Today these people still believe in the strength and wonder of the wolf. May we benefit from the wisdom of the nuu-chah-nulth . . . before a friend, a wild brother is lost to us forever.

guide to pronunciation

Nuu-chah-nulth (new-cha-nulth) last syllable sounds like "tooth" with an N and L
tsumh (tay-sum)
Kwaht-yaht (kwhat-yacht) first syllable pronounced like "what" with a K in front
Kloo-kwalah (clue-qual-la) "qual" pronounced as in the word, "quality"

Squeals and laughter of the children filled the tiny attic. The old man, sitting in his chair on the floor below, looked at the ceiling and smiled. The sounds of his grandchildren were happy sounds. Suddenly one of the children shouted: "tsumh!" At once the house was quiet. The old man waited.

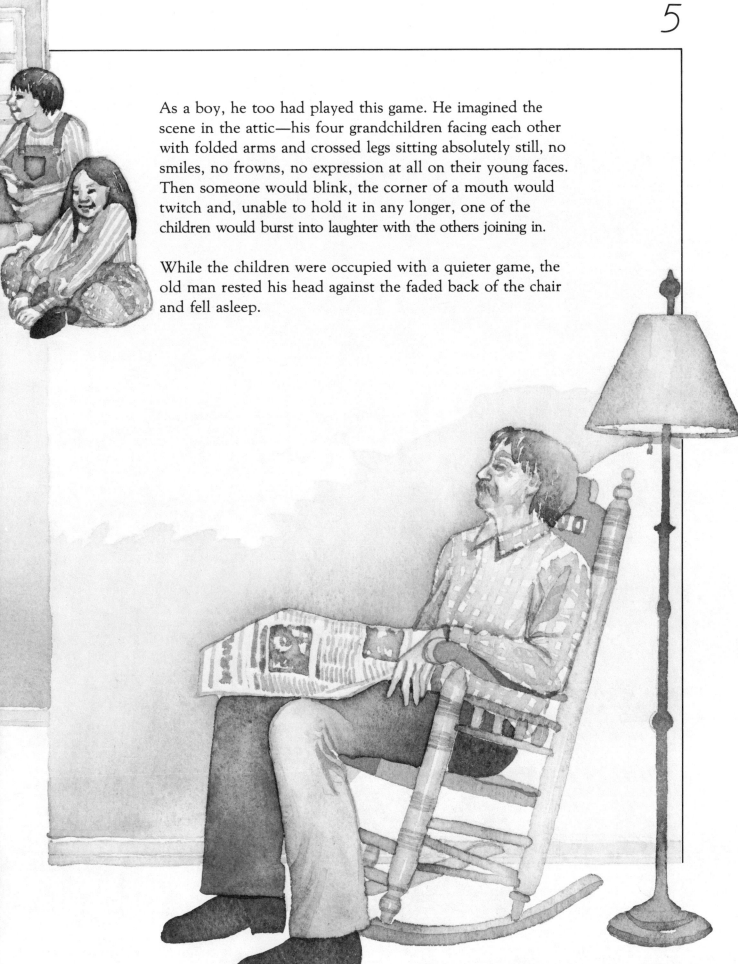

As a boy, he too had played this game. He imagined the scene in the attic—his four grandchildren facing each other with folded arms and crossed legs sitting absolutely still, no smiles, no frowns, no expression at all on their young faces. Then someone would blink, the corner of a mouth would twitch and, unable to hold it in any longer, one of the children would burst into laughter with the others joining in.

While the children were occupied with a quieter game, the old man rested his head against the faded back of the chair and fell asleep.

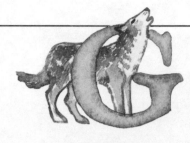

"Grandfather, grandfather, look what we have found!"

The old man awoke with a start.

The four children pounded down the narrow staircase leading from the attic. The first child carried in his arms something large and long. It was made of wood and had the face of an animal. Its large eyes were painted black; the end of its long snout was rounded and black; and its many teeth

were white. Long, brown strands of soft cedar bark swung from the top of its head. The small child staggered under its weight. The old man caught his breath, for as the child felt for the last step, he stumbled and the wooden mask crashed to the floor.

With a cry the old man jumped to his feet. He ran to the mask and gathered it gently into his arms. The lines of his wrinkled face deepened and his eyes flared with anger. "You have shamed me by your behavior. Have I not taught you respect for the 'old things?'" The old man rubbed the wooden muzzle. "Go home. Tell your parents what you have done."

Heads lowered, the children left the house and gently closed the door behind them.

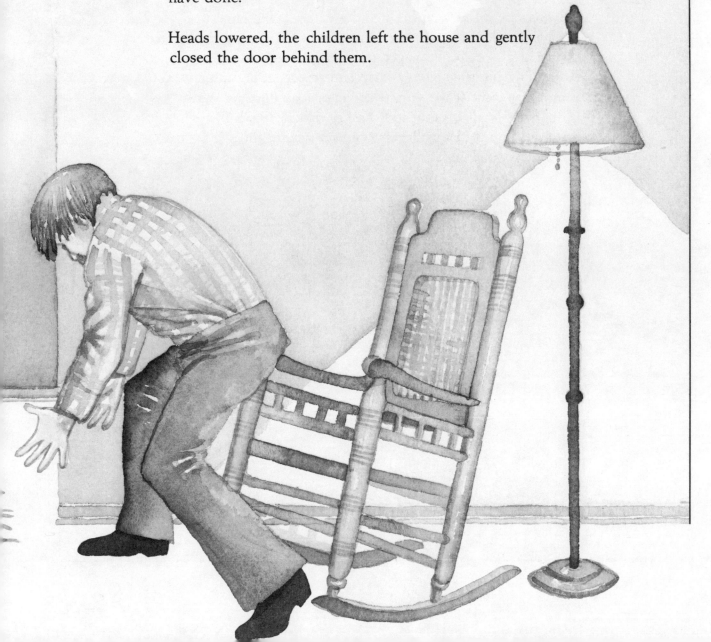

The old man grunted with the effort of climbing the stairs. Slowly he made his way to the back of the cluttered, musty attic. With a sigh he sat down in a worn chair and cradled the mask in his arms. He closed his eyes and softly hummed a song of his people. He stroked the rough wood of the mask, and old memories spoke to him. With a smile, he remembered a special day years ago when he was a boy. He turned his head to the side; he could almost hear the taunting voices of his friends as they searched for him that day . . .

"Kwaht-yaht is bald!" the dark-haired children shouted.

"Aw, come on, let's go back to the village," the largest of the boys said. "He will never give away such a good hiding spot. He has probably played another trick on us. Remember the time we searched and searched, and then found him back at the village? He is probably eating sweet blueberries from his mother's basket right now while we sweat in the sun. He will not fool us a second time."

In his hiding place, Kwaht-yaht covered his mouth so that he would not laugh out loud and give himself away. He watched as the children turned their backs on him and trudged away in the sand.

When they were well out of sight, Kwaht-yaht crawled out of his hiding place and shook the sand from his shoulder-length black hair. He stretched and walked to the water's edge. He waded into the surf. It was icy cold even in the middle of the summer.

Kwaht-yaht loved this time of the year. In spring the people moved from their winter village to the outside beaches. Their long wooden houses lined the banks, and their slender, cedar canoes graced the shoreline.

Kwaht-yaht's people lived a good life. They seldom went hungry. The land and sea were rich with food.

The boy waded back to the shore and sat down in the warm sand. He liked the games and races of other boys, but today his thoughts were his companions.

waht-yaht was the only son of a chief. As a chief, his father did not paddle his own canoe. To celebrate special occasions (like births, marriages, name-givings), Kwaht-yaht's father gave elaborate potlatches. A potlatch lasted for several days, and was a time of feasting, gift-giving, dancing and storytelling.

Someday, Kwaht-yaht too would be a chief. To prepare him, his father told many stories of his people. Kwaht-yaht loved the stories. There were many tales of animals, of raven, bear and wolf. To the people, wolves were special. The wolves were a tribe. They lived in a village under a mountain. In their houses under the mountain they removed their fur coats and lived as people.

One day Kwaht-yaht asked his father, "What makes a great chief?"

His father slowly raised his head and put aside his carving. Kwaht-yaht was his only child, and he loved him deeply. Kwaht-yaht's father said, "Look to the wolf for guidance. The wolf is a good hunter. Seeking food for his family, the wolf may travel for days while his stomach groans with hunger. Yet, his nose and eyes and ears remain keen. He sees the twitch of the elk's ear in the forest; he hears the scratching of the mouse in his house under the ground.

"Someday, Kwaht-yaht, you will go to sea in a tiny canoe and harpoon the whale in order to feed your people. You will be tired and thirsty and hungry, but like the wolf your suffering must make you strong.

"The wolf's strength is not of one, but of five or six or seven wolves. The wolf does not hunt alone; he hunts with other members of his family.

"Wolves depend upon each other. When they travel through deep snow they take turns making a path for the others to follow. A good leader, Kwaht-yaht, must also at times be a good follower.

"Like the wolf, be generous. After the wolf and his family eat at their kill, then birds and other animals come to feast. Raven, crow and eagle, bear, and mountain lion eat what the wolf leaves behind."

Kwaht-yaht's father looked up at the sky. "Raven and wolf share something special. Raven follows wolf to his kill. If wolf travels at night when raven cannot follow, in the morning the black bird will be guided by the wolf's own tracks. It is clear that wolf feeds raven, but what does raven do for wolf? I think that raven makes wolf laugh."

Kwaht-yaht's father looked serious. "Wolf guards his den against his enemies. He watches the sky for eagle who will carry away the pups. He stands with his family against bear who would steal the meat that wolf hides at his den for his young. Like wolf, you must protect your children and your people from your enemies. One day Kwaht-yaht you will own all that I have; my streams and berry patches, my songs and masks. You must protect these things as I have, so that your children and grandchildren will own them too.

"The wolf keeps peace within his own family. Wolves are powerful animals. If they were to fight often among themselves, they would grow weak for the hunt. As I have taught you from birth, Kwaht-yaht, a chief turns his back on mean words, and never quarrels."

Kwaht-yaht's father smiled. "Yet, in spite of his burdens, wolf never forgets to play with his children."

Kwaht-yaht's young face was serious as he thought of his father's words. He hoped that someday he would be as good and wise as he. Kwaht-yaht stood up and spat the spruce gum from his mouth. "All this thinking has made my gum grow old," he said to himself. "The sun will soon be gone. I will go into the forest and scrape another piece of sap from the spruce tree."

As the boy covered the short distance from the shoreline to the edge of the forest, his thoughts turned again to wolves. One day soon—perhaps in this year's winter village—he would be initiated into the tribe through the wolf ritual called Kloo-kwalah.

Late at night when the moon was full, he would be asleep, and the "wolves" would come for him. These human wolves would paint their faces, arms and legs black. They would wear black or gray blankets. They would tie one corner of the blankets, and place them over their heads so that the tied corners looked like the snouts or noses of wolves. (The beautiful wolf masks would be worn later by the dancers.)

Kwaht-yaht would not be afraid. Through stories, his parents and grandparents had prepared him for the ritual. It would be a great honor.

The human "wolves" would whistle and howl and beat upon the wooden sides of the house. They would take the boards from the back of the house, and crawl through the holes they had made. Small children would whimper and mothers would draw them close. The "wolves" would run about the room, and overturn anything in their path. And then as quickly as they had come—they would be gone. The parents of the house would go about setting things right. It was then they would discover that some of their children were missing.

The human "wolves" would take the children to the forest and there they would teach them the dances and songs and give them the masks that it was their right to have. The ceremony would last for four days, and of course the "wolves" would return the children to their parents. There would be dancing and singing and feasting, and at the end, the youngsters would be full members of the Kloo-kwalah society and would carry with them the "strength of the wolf."

Kwaht-yaht entered the forest and searched about for a spruce tree. Finally, he found one where pitch dripped from a scar on the tree. His mouth watered for the tasty sap and he began to work at it with his fingernail.

Snap! A branch cracked under the weight of a foot? A paw?

Kwaht-yaht looked around, but was not concerned. His people did not fear the forest as some tribes did. From visitors he had heard stories of dangerous forest spirits—of dwarfs who lured people to their dwellings inside of mountains. There were tales of birds who had the faces of men and a creature like a mountain lion that traveled backwards and swinging its horrible spearlike tail struck down humans.

Suddenly Kwaht-yaht whirled around at the sound of a muffled sneeze. And then he saw the sight that he would never forget in all of his long life. There in the fading light stood a great gray wolf. The wolf's rounded ears were forward, his furry tail waved gently from side to side and his mouth opened in what almost looked like a smile.

The boy did not move, or blink or even take a breath. Kwaht-yaht met the wolf's yellow stare. And in the eyes of the wolf the boy saw a great hunter who fed his family, a chief who kept peace in his own tribe, and a father who protected, and taught and played with his children. Kwaht-yaht returned his wild brother's smile.

The magic lasted for only a heartbeat, and then the wolf was gone . . .

The old man shivered in the attic; it had grown cold and damp with the setting sun. He looked at the wolf mask resting in his lap. Would his grandchildren remember the songs and dances of the people? Would they love this mask and its past as he had?

He ran his hands through his hair. Where had the afternoon gone? Suddenly he felt very old and sad.

Sighing, the old man straightened and put the wolf mask back in its place. Its eyes stared at him.

Speaking softly to the mask, he said, "How I miss the old ways, my friend. Time held us both more gently then."

"Grandfather . . . grandfather."

The old man squinted hard in the dim light of the attic to find the source of the small, tear-choked cry.

"Kwaht-yaht, what are you doing here?" It was the old man's youngest grandchild. This handsome, wide-eyed boy had been given his grandfather's name.

"I'm sorry about the wolf mask." The dirty little face was streaked with tears. "When I am older, grandfather, I will make wonderful masks just for you."

A smile brightened the old man's face. He bent down and drew the boy close to him. Gently, he wiped the tears from the boy's cheeks. "Yes, I will sing the songs and teach you the stories of our family. When I am gone, Kwaht-yaht, you will remember and you will carve beautiful masks. Through the songs and stories and your masks, the strength of the wolf will live forever in our people."

THE
END

? Why is a wolf made the way it is? Build a wolf and find out.

materials

scissors, crayons or markers, tape or paste, blank sheet of paper.

directions

1 Cut out the bodies, legs and feet, tails, necks and heads, and muzzles from the patterns on pages 21 and 29. (4 pieces)

2 Arrange them on a flat surface so that all parts are visible. (Keep bodies, legs, heads, etc. grouped together.)

3 Read the following characteristics. Choose the correct body part and "build a wolf!"

● BODY AND FUR
■ A wolf's body is strong and powerful.
■ The wolf's beautiful coat is made up of two layers of fur. The underfur is short, soft and thick. It is covered by longer, stiff guard hairs to keep the underfur dry.

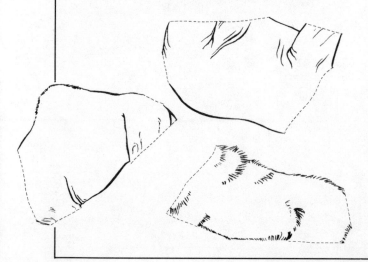

● TAIL
■ Wolves have long, furry tails. They use their tails to communicate. They also use them to stay warm. In winter when they curl up to sleep, they tuck their muzzle between their back legs and their tails cover their faces. At temperatures far below zero, they can sleep snuggly.

● NECK AND HEAD
■ The wolf's neck is short and muscular and its head is wide.
■ A wolf's ears are erect ("stand up").
■ The ears are short. They are not as affected by the cold as long ears. Wolves that live in warmer places tend to have longer ears that give off excess heat.
■ By shifting their ears from side to side, wolves can determine from what direction a sound is coming.
Wolves have good eyesight.

continued on next page...

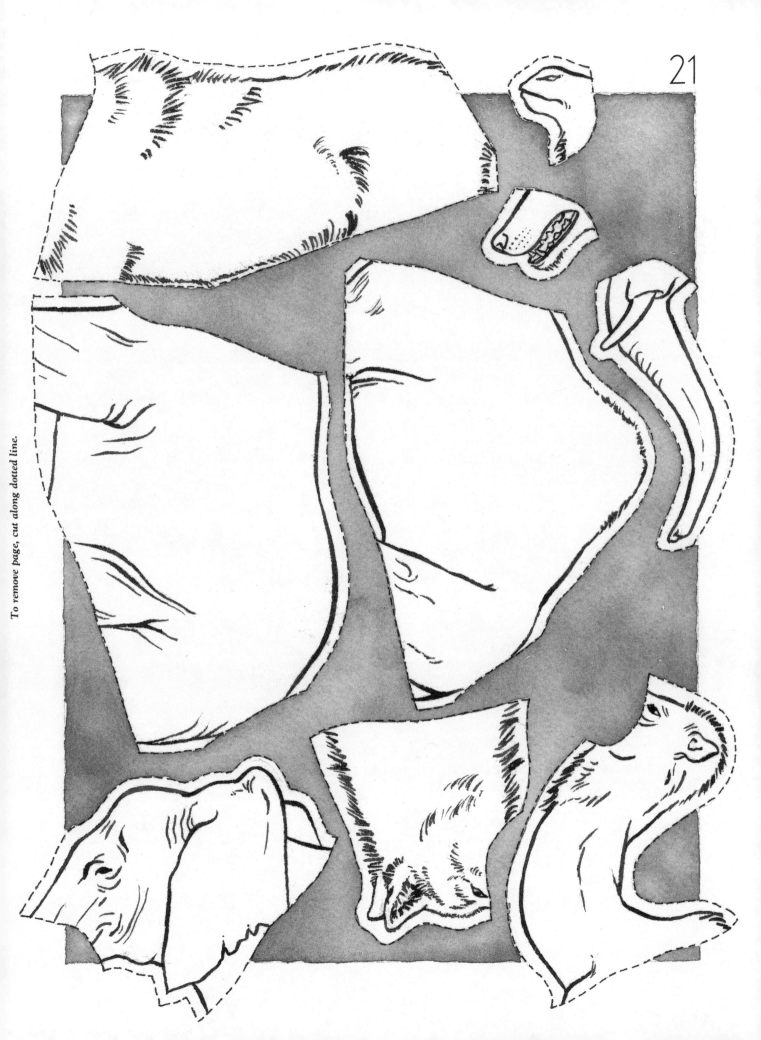

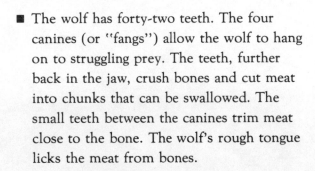

■ The wolf has forty-two teeth. The four canines (or "fangs") allow the wolf to hang on to struggling prey. The teeth, further back in the jaw, crush bones and cut meat into chunks that can be swallowed. The small teeth between the canines trim meat close to the bone. The wolf's rough tongue licks the meat from bones.

● LEGS AND FEET

■ The four legs of wolves are long and muscular. Wolves walk and run on their toes. This adds length to the leg. The long legs give them greater speed and allow them to move through deep snow.

■ Wolves have large, blocky feet. When their feet touch the ground, their toes spread out. The wolf's feet act like "snowshoes" allowing the animal to walk on snow or ice without breaking through.

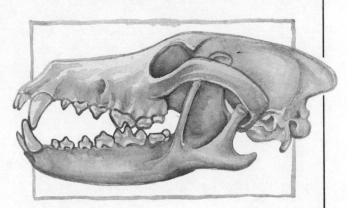

■ With the "tools" to do all these different things, the wolf eats almost every part of the prey animal. There is no waste.

● MUZZLE (SNOUT)

■ Over time wolves have developed broad, long, heavy muzzles for the purpose of hunting large animals.

■ Because of the two hundred million "smelling cells" in the wolf's large nose, a wolf can smell about a hundred times better than a person.

■ The large jaws provide a place of attachment for the strong chewing muscles.

4 When you have completed your wolf, glue the parts to a piece of paper and color it.

5 Read the characteristics again and draw a picture of a wolf.

6 JUST FOR FUN: Mix up all of the body parts. Create your own imaginary animal. Draw a picture of where this "crazy critter" lives. Give him a name and write or tell a story about him.

Build-A-Wolf patterns continued on page 29

In the story, Kwaht-yaht looked forward to seeing the dancers wearing the wolf mask at the Kloo-kwalah ceremony. Make your own wolf mask to wear.

materials

markers or crayons, scissors, glue, straw, raffia, string or yarn.

directions

1 Carefully pull the mask (pages 25 to 29) from the book, keeping them in one piece.

2 Color mask.

3 Cut out on the dotted lines.

4 Fold down the sides of the mask along the heavy black lines.

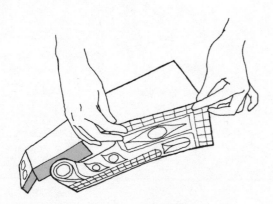

5 Fold in the shaded tabs.

6 Glue the tabs to the sections inside the mask where indicated, (tab A to section A, tab B to section B and tab C to section C).

7 Glue on straw, raffia, string or yarn to the top.

Wear on top of your head like a hat.

activity

● Put on your wolf mask. Imagine that you are a great gray wolf. All around you is your territory—your home. Look through the eyes of the wolf. What do you see? Draw it.

Mask pattern designed by Melanie Mitchell.

SECTION A

SECTION A

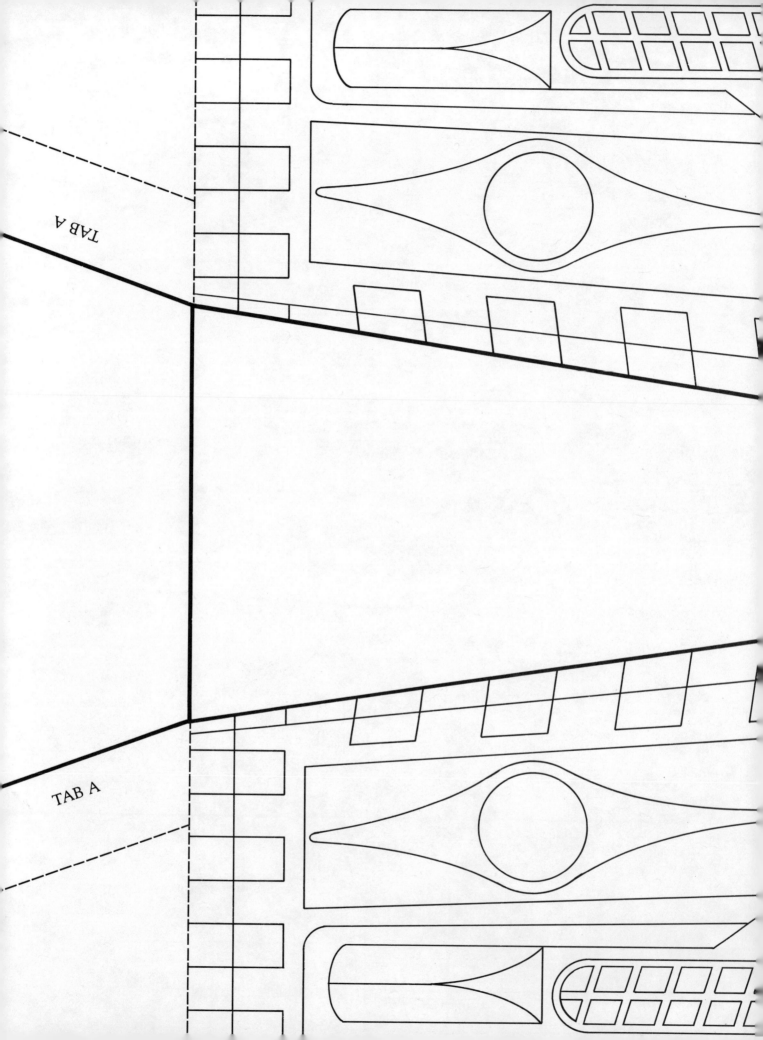

TAB A

TAB A

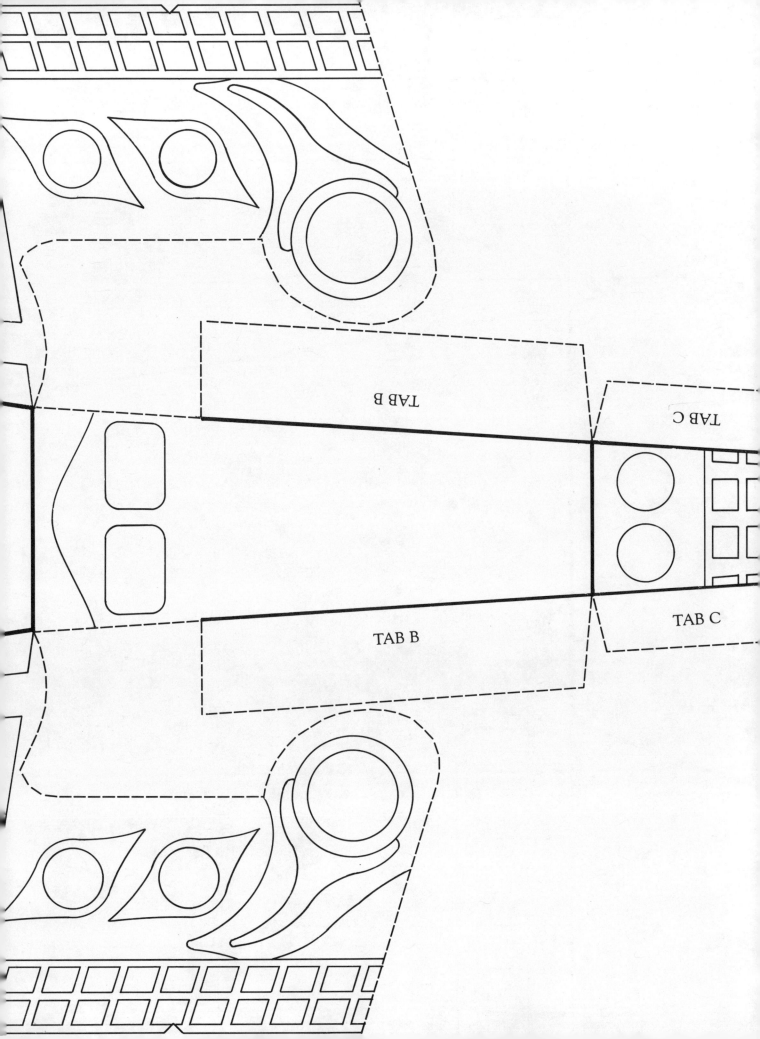

TAB B

TAB C

TAB B

TAB C

SECTION B

SECTION
C

SECTION
C

SECTION B

To remove page, cut along dotted line.

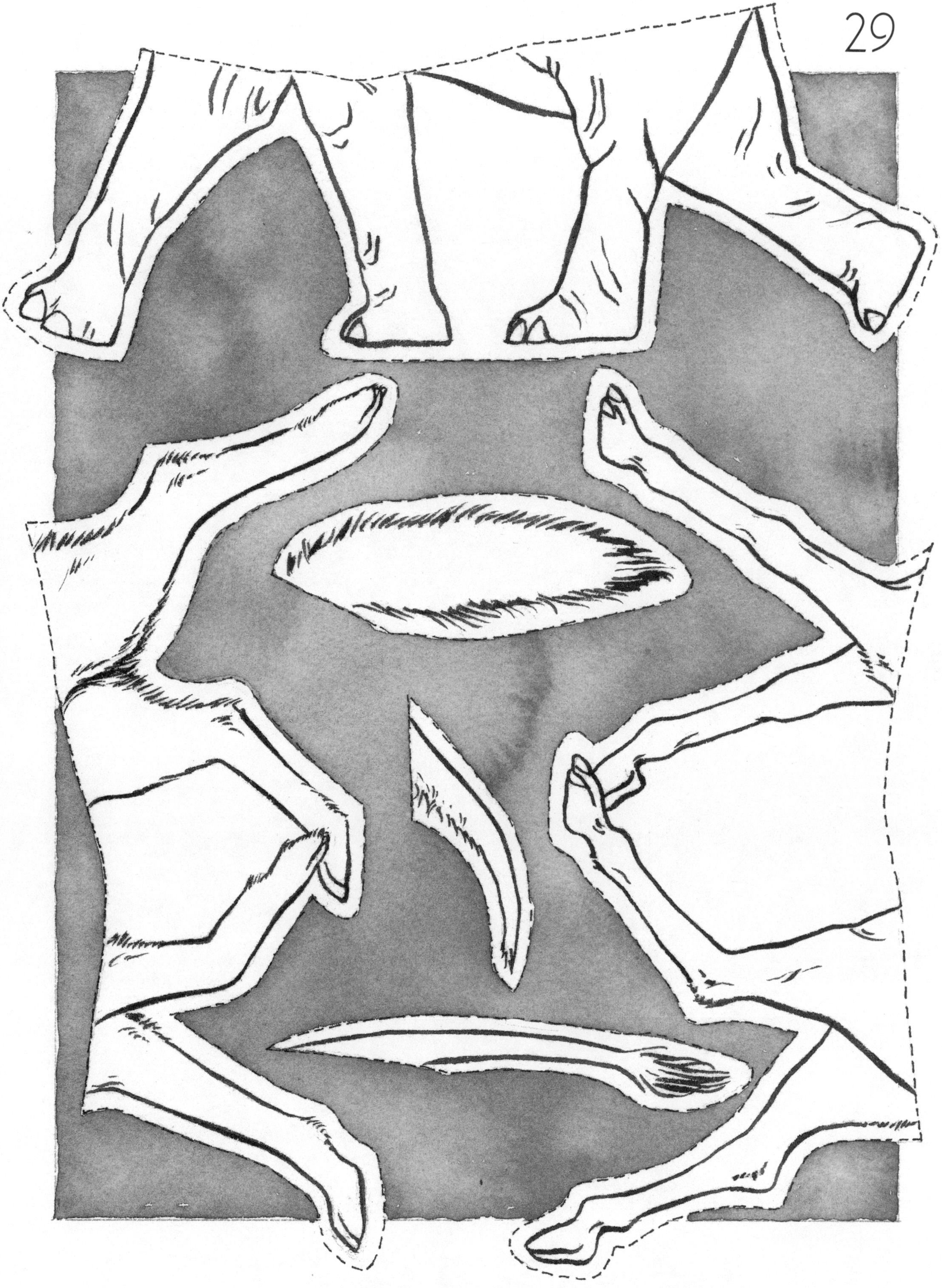

In the BUILD-A-WOLF activity, we discussed what a wolf looks like on the "outside." Now, let's have the wolf take off his coat, and see how he looks on the "inside." The West Coast people believed that when a wolf took off his fur coat, he was a person underneath. What do you see "underneath?"

activity

● Hold this page up to the light, and you will see the skeleton of the wolf.

A wolf (from the tip of his nose to the end of his tail) is almost as long as a man is tall.

continued on next page...

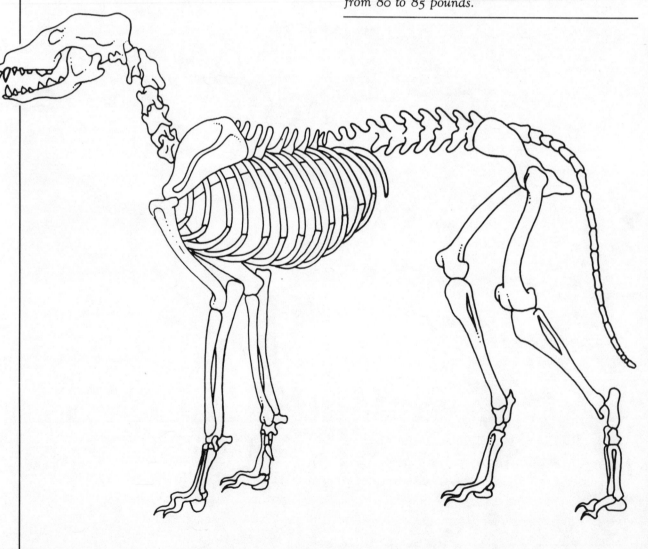

- The scientific name for the wolf is *Canis lupus*. The scientific name for your dog is *Canis familiaris*. The ancestors of all dogs (from toy poodles to German shepherds) are wolves. All of the qualities (loyalty, playfulness and intelligence) that we love in our pet dogs came from wolves.

- Members of the dog family (Canidae) include the wolf, coyote, fox, jackal and your pet dog (whether it is a Chihuahua or a German shepherd.)

Average adult male wolves weigh from 95 to 100 pounds. Average adult female wolves weigh from 80 to 85 pounds.

Have you ever sung the song, "There were ten in the bed and the little one said, 'Roll over, roll over. . . ' If you have, you know that the nine children continue "rolling over" until only the little one is left in bed.

- In a way this is what has happened to the wolf and other animals throughout the world. In the song there is only one bed for all of the children. Likewise, there is only one world for people and wildlife to share. Sometimes humans are selfish. Often we have been the little child in the bed who sings, "Roll over, roll over." And each time we have rolled over, another species has been forced "out of the bed" (that is, off of the land).

- An animal that has been forced out of the bed is said to be EXTINCT. A species of animal becomes extinct when every individual of its kind is dead. Extinctions have occurred since the beginning of life on earth. Dinosaurs are extinct. However, in the past 350 years, extinctions have been taking place at a rapid rate. There has not been time for new species to develop and replace the ones that have died off. So, the variety of plants and animals on earth is being reduced.

- If an animal is on the very edge of the bed, we say that species of animal is ENDANGERED. This means that humans must protect these animals or else they will slip into extinction.

- Animals that are THREATENED are approaching the edge of the bed. They may be plentiful in some parts of the world, but overall their populations are being reduced.

- Two species of wolf live in North America:

  Canis rufus, the red wolf, and

Canis lupus, the gray wolf.

The red wolf once was listed as extinct in the wild. However, some animals still survived in captivity. In 1987 red wolves were restored to a national wildlife refuge in North Carolina, and so far they are doing well.

continued on next page...

■ At one time, wolves roamed almost all of North America. SEE MAP. In fact, throughout the world wolves have lived in grasslands, swamps, forests, mountains, deserts and even parts of the frozen north.

■ Today, throughout much of North America the night-music of the wolf is only a memory. In 48 states the gray wolf is listed as an endangered species. In Northern Minnesota it is classified as threatened. Plans are being drafted to restore gray wolves to certain parts of the country. The success of these recovery plans and the survival of the wolf depend upon people's willingness to share. We certainly would not want to continue "rolling over" until there was no one left—but ourselves.

activity

● Look at the map on the opposite page. This is a map of North America. Discuss these questions with your parents or friends.

1 Where is the United States of America on this map?

2 What is the name of the state in which you live? Find it on the map. Point out about where you live in your state.

3 Are there wolves where you live today? Did wolves ever roam the area where you live?

The dog family evolved in North America and Europe and over time spread to other areas.

4 What human activities have forced wolves off of the land?
(Suggested answer: the hunting, trapping and poisoning of wolves have greatly reduced their numbers. Wolf habitat has been destroyed by the cutting of forests, development and pollution. If people were to decide against the wolf, modern man could poison them and hunt them from helicopters and planes and thus destroy the last wolves on earth within ten years.)

5 Do you believe that people can learn to share the land?
(Suggested answer: there are concerned and caring people all over the world who are working hard to insure that wildlife will have its "fair share."
An informed and caring person can make a difference. You can be that person!)

6 HOW CAN YOU HELP?

Express your opinion! Write a letter to the President of the United States and express your feelings about sharing the land with wildlife. Request a response.

Ask your parents to write a letter. Organize your friends in a letter-writing campaign!

Range = the region in which an animal lives. At one time, wolf tracks could be found in almost all of North America. Would you believe a wolf lived where New York City now stands? It's hard to imagine!

Gray Wolf
current range

Gray Wolf
former range

Red Wolf
restored

Red Wolf
former range

Wolves may be rare or endangered where you live, but through origami, create your own wolf pack.

Origami or "paper folding" is a Japanese art form dating back to about 1682.

materials

- You may use any size paper, but it must be square. Lightweight paper is easier to crease; newspaper works fine.

- You may use any color paper, but wolves are generally black, white, or gray. Pups born to the same parents at the same time may differ in color.

- The color of the wolf's coat often blends with the surroundings in which the animal lives.

How many wolves should you make, that is, how many animals are generally in a wolf pack?

- The number varies. Packs usually have 5-8 family members. However, packs can be as small as two or as large as thirty animals.

- In every pack there is a leader—the ALPHA animal. Quite often there are an alpha male and female. (The alpha male is usually dominant to the alpha female.) This pair decides the pack's activities. Generally, only the alpha pair breed and produce pups. However, the entire pack hunts and cares for the pups.

directions

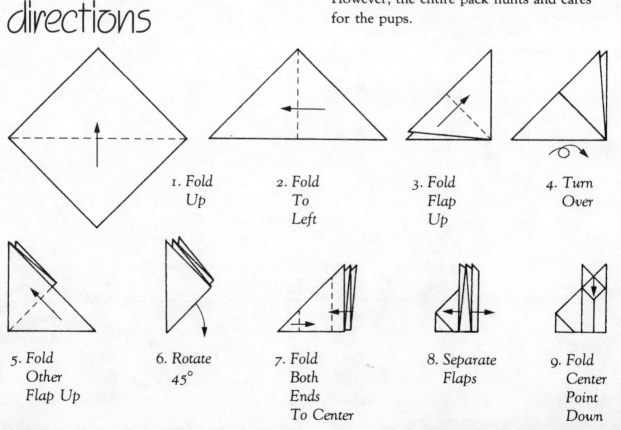

1. Fold Up
2. Fold To Left
3. Fold Flap Up
4. Turn Over
5. Fold Other Flap Up
6. Rotate 45°
7. Fold Both Ends To Center
8. Separate Flaps
9. Fold Center Point Down

Pattern published with permission of its creator, MR. MITSUO OKUDA, from his original design, 'Seated Fox,' retitled, 'Gray Wolf.'

- The alpha animal is sometimes challenged by another pack member. The challenger may defeat the alpha animal and become the leader himself. Or he may leave the pack and become a LONER, seeking another wolf with whom he may start his own pack.

- A wolf pack is like a successful football team—every "player" has a certain position. The alpha animal is like the quarterback who calls the plays. A wolf pack that "wins" is a pack that works together as a team and "survives."

their pups. (Wolves often dig their own dens, or they may occupy abandoned beaver dams, hollow logs or holes left by other animals.) If left alone, wolves will use the same den for several years.

- This type of habitat would attract not only wolves but also other animals that could be food for the wolf.

- A wolf pack lives and hunts in a certain area that it also defends against other wolves. This area is called a TERRITORY. The size of a territory varies.

...AND HABITAT

After you have finished folding your wolf pack, turn the page to the "habitat." Study these pages for just a moment.

- Why would this make an excellent wolf habitat?

- Think of what you need to live: food, water, shelter. A wolf needs very similar things. Trees and shrubs provide excellent "cover"—affording protection from the sun in summer, and wind and snow in winter. The stream is a source of water.

- The hill in the foreground of the picture gives the wolf a "look-out." The high, dry rock cave is a good place for wolves to raise

activity

- Color the wolf's habitat.

- With the book open to the habitat pages, stand it up. Pretend that this is your wolf pack's territory. Using your origami wolves, play "wolf family." Select the alpha animals. Who will be the mother of the pups? What will your wolf pack hunt for food?

- Look very closely and see if you can find the animals "hiding" in this picture. How good a hunter are you?

Answers on page 52.

The wolf can be described as social, intelligent and adaptable, with strong family bonds.

continued on next page...

Wolves COMMUNICATE or "share information." Communication takes place between members of a pack and among different packs.

How do wolves communicate with each other? Wolves use their eyes, ears, mouths, fur and tails (in fact, all of themselves) to share information and even feelings.

■ Let's try "talkin' wolf." Your stomach is full, you're rested, and it's a cool, crisp fall day. You feel good! You want to play.

■ But how do you communicate this to one of your pack members? Simple! You bow, that is, you PLAY BOW.

■ In a play bow, the wolf extends its two front legs and raises its hindquarters. Its tail is wagging, its ears are up, and it is wearing a PLAY GRIN. A play grin is a big open-mouthed "smile." The wolf is often panting. When it jumps onto the pack member with whom it wants to play, the wolf will know that this grinning, panting animal does not want to fight. It's all in fun!

■ A behavior that you may recognize from your own dog is the GREETING CEREMONY. When the leader returns to the pack or when the wolves wake up from a rest they will gather around the alpha animal and lick or gently grasp its muzzle. In this "ceremony" the wolves may be saying, "You are our leader, you are like a father to us" or they may be communicating, "We're hungry, let's hunt."

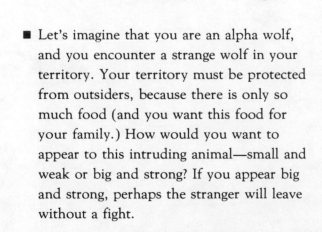

■ Let's imagine that you are an alpha wolf, and you encounter a strange wolf in your territory. Your territory must be protected from outsiders, because there is only so much food (and you want this food for your family.) How would you want to appear to this intruding animal—small and weak or big and strong? If you appear big and strong, perhaps the stranger will leave without a fight.

■ With your whole body, you "tell" the stranger "to go away." You tense your legs and make yourself look as tall as possible.

■ The fur on your back and tail stands up. Your ears are up and forward and you stare directly at this intruder. Your lips are raised and you display your "weapons"—your teeth.

■ The stranger gets the message and leaves. You relax. But that exchange was stressful and dangerous.

■ To avoid such "meetings," wolves communicate by SCENT MARKING. They mark their territories by urinating on rocks, trees, etc. One sniff of a marked tree tells an "outsider" that this is not an odor of his family, and that he is trespassing.

■ Wolves also communicate by howling. Howling may occur day or night and allows pack members to locate each other when they are separated. It pulls the family together before and after a hunt, and serves as an alarm. It is a warning to outsiders; it alerts other wolf packs and lone wolves that this territory is taken. Scientists still do not know all the reasons that wolves howl— sometimes they seem to do it just for the joy of it!

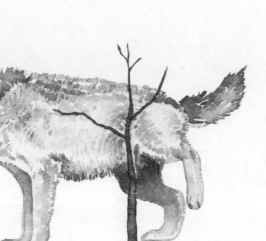

● The following chart on page 42 will aid you in "talkin' wolf."

■ Not only wolves but also we "two-legs" use our bodies to share feelings and information. We cross our arms and by doing so say, "don't get too close." We rub the top of our noses when we are puzzled. We drum our fingers on a desk top when we are tired of waiting. We do not always smile out of happiness. Sometimes we smile to say, "I'm sorry, I did not mean to bump into you."

continued on next page...

MESSAGE	HEAD	TAIL	OTHER
"I Want To Play"	Ears Forward Play Grin	Up And Wagging	"Play Bow"
"You Are My Leader; You Are My Superior"	Head Lowered Ears Back Tense Grin Eyes Averted	Down—Often Tucked Between Hind Legs	Fur Is Flat To Make Itself Look Smaller
"I Am The Leader"	Head High Ears Forward Mouth Relaxed Direct Stare	Held High	Fur Fluffed, Animal Is Relaxed
"Don't Hurt Me; I Don't Want To Fight."	Head Down Ears Back Mouth Closed Eyes Averted	Low—Often Tucked	Animal Rolls On Back And Shows His Belly

activity

- In the following game, you will discover how you use your body to communicate your feelings. Take turns. Use the situations below or make up your own.

- Read the situation and just using your body—no voices—act out how you would feel. Were your actions always clear to the person watching you? Discuss your feelings with your parents.

1 You wake up in the middle of the night and hear a strange, frightening noise. How do you feel? (You discover it was only the wind blowing through a window that had been left partially open. Now, how do you feel?)

2 Finally, it is recess. You have made up a game that you want your friends to play with you. But they decide to play someone else's game. How do you feel?

3 You find out your best friend is moving away. How do you feel?

4 Your parent stops what she is doing and asks, "How would you like to play a game or read a book?" How do you feel?

5 Your parent puts his arms around you and says, "You're the best kid in the whole world." How do you feel?

There are few places left in North America where a person can see wolves in the wild. Because of their shy nature, wolves are difficult to see in the wilderness. Many people who have spent years hiking in wolf country have never seen a wolf.

- However, you and your family may be closer to a wolf than you think. On page 45 you will find a list of zoos that have captive wolves. Plan to visit one of these areas.
- Take along your wolf book, and use the wolf observation form on the next page.

- For practice, study the wolves below and record your observations.
- The best time to observe wolves in a zoo is early morning or late afternoon. In general, wolves are more active in winter than in summer and are more aroused on windy than calm days.

continued on next page...

● At the zoo, study all of the animals for a few minutes and then select *one* that is easy for you to recognize.

1 What sets this animal apart from the others? Does one of its ears droop? Does it have any special markings? Is it a different color? Does it have a scar? Describe what makes your animal "special": _____

_____

_____

_____

_____

_____

2 How does your wolf hold its ears most of the time?

_____ Forward

_____ Laid Back

_____ In the Middle

3 How does your wolf hold its tail most of the time?

_____ High

_____ Low

_____ Between Its Back Legs

4 How does your wolf look at other wolves?

_____ Stares At Them

_____ Does Not Look Directly At Others

5 In comparison to other wolves in the pack, does your wolf give the impression of being larger or smaller? Does it try to make itself appear smaller or larger by keeping its fur flat or fluffing its fur?

_____ Larger

_____ Smaller

6 How does it hold its mouth?

_____ Easy, Open-Mouthed Grin

_____ Lips Pulled Back, Teeth Showing

7 In general, does your wolf seem relaxed or more tense around other wolves?

_____ Relaxed _____ Tense

8 Does your wolf make any sounds during the observation period?

_____ Growls _____ Whimpers

_____ Sneezes _____ Howls

9 If you did see a greeting ceremony, was your wolf the center of all the fuss or was it one of the wolves to nuzzle the pack leader?

_____ Center

_____ Trying To Nuzzle Main Wolf

10 Did your wolf at any time roll over and show its side or belly or throat to another wolf?

_____ No _____ Yes

11 From your observations, do you think that your animal is an "alpha" animal or a subordinate animal?

Look over the information on your form. If most of your checks were for the first answer (questions #2, 3, 4, 5, 6, 7, 9, 10), then your special wolf was probably the "alpha" wolf.

If your answer to number 10 was yes, then your wolf was a subordinate animal.

Alpha Wolf? _____ Yes _____ No

12 On another sheet, draw a picture of your wolf. If you have the opportunity, ask the zoo keeper if you were correct in determining that your animal was (or was not) the alpha animal. If you observed the wolf on the previous page, check the answer key.

13 If you have your camera with you, take a picture of your wolf.

● With your photographs, drawings and observations, you may want to make a scrapbook of your special wolf.

SOME ZOOS WHERE GRAY OR RED WOLVES MAY BE SEEN

GRAY WOLVES

Alameda Park Zoo, Alamogordo, New Mexico
Arizona-Sonora Desert Museum, Tucson, Arizona
Audubon Park Zoo, New Orleans, Louisiana
Beardsley Park Zoo, Bridgeport, Connecticut
Binder Park Zoo, Battle Creek, Michigan
Brookfield Zoo, Chicago, Illinois
Burnet Zoo, Syracuse, New York
Calgary Zoo, Calgary, Alberta, Canada
Carlos Avery Wolf Sanctuary, Forest Lake, Minnesota
Columbus Zoological Gardens, Columbus, Ohio
Denver Zoological Garden, Denver, Colorado
Detroit Zoological Park, Royal Oak, Michigan
Fresno Park Zoo, Fresno, California
Great Plains Zoo, Sioux Falls, South Dakota
Lincoln Park Zoological Gardens, Chicago, Illinois
Living Desert State Park, Carlsbad, New Mexico
Los Angeles Zoo, Los Angeles, California
Mesker Park Zoo, Evansville, Indiana
Metro Toronto Zoo, Toronto, Canada
Milwaukee County Zoo, Milwaukee, Wisconsin
Minnesota Zoological Garden, Apple Valley, Minnesota
Moorpark College-Inst. W & E Animals, California
National Zoological Park, Washington, D.C.
New York Zoological Park, Bronx, New York
Northwest Trek Wildlife Park, Eatonville, Washington
Philadelphia Zoological Gardens, Philadelphia, Pennsylvania
Phoenix Zoo, Phoenix, Arizona
Potter Park Zoo, Lansing, Michigan
Quebec-Jardin Zoologique De, Orsainville, Quebec
Racine Zoological Garden, Racine, Wisconsin
Rio Grande Zoo, Albuquerque, New Mexico
Roger Williams Park Zoo, Providence, Rhode Island
Roosevelt Park Zoo, Minot, North Dakota
Ross Park Zoo, Binghamton, New York
San Diego Zoological Garden, San Diego, California
San Francisco Zoo, San Francisco, California
Seneca Park Zoo, Rochester, New York
Stanley Park Zoo, Vancouver, British Columbia
St. Paul's Como Zoo, St. Paul, Minnesota
Tulsa Zoological Park, Tulsa, Oklahoma
Washington Park Zoo, Portland, Oregon
Wild Canid Survival and Research Center, Eureka, Missouri
Wildlife Safari, Inc., Winston, Oregon
Wolf Park, Battle Ground, Indiana

RED WOLVES

Alexandria Zoological Park, Alexandria, Louisiana
Audubon Park Zoo, New Orleans, Louisiana
Burnet Zoo, Syracuse, New York
Greater Baton Rouge Zoo, Baton Rouge, Louisiana
Oglebay Good Children's Zoo, Wheeling, West Virginia
Point Defiance Zoo and Aquarium, Tacoma, Washington
Wild Canid Survival and Research Center, Eureka, Missouri
Wolf Park, Battle Ground, Indiana

*There are additional facilities that maintain wolves. This list was compiled through ISIS (International Species Inventory System). In planning a visit to one of the areas listed above, call in advance to confirm that wolves are still being exhibited.

What do kids and wolves have in common? Among a number of things, kids and wolves love to play! Play is important for all animals. While playing, we are also learning.

- Wolf pups wrestle and chase each other in a kind of tag. At the age of three weeks pups in a litter begin "play-fighting" among themselves. When they are thirty days old, the pups may begin to fight for real. They will struggle for a number of days until one pup rolls on its back, and by showing its belly, says, "I give up."

- Pups play not only among themselves, but also with adults. Pups will crawl all over an adult and will pull at its tail and bite its ears until the adult, by standing up and shaking, indicates, "I can't take any more of this!" Adult wolves are very gentle and loving with pups.

- Like pups, the adults wrestle and play tag. A wolf communicates his desire to play by "play bowing."

activity

1 Use this time together to play a game with your parent. Select one of your favorite games or play "tsumh," (tay-sum). Tsumh, a game of the West Coast people, is described at the beginning of the story, "The Mask of the Wolf."

2 To play "tsumh," you and your parent will sit on the floor with your legs and arms crossed. Shout the word, "tsumh!"

3 Wipe all expression from your faces. Stare at each other and don't budge! Whoever moves or laughs first loses! Play the game a number of times and involve other family members. Who is the tsumh champion in your family?

- Grown wolves appear to enjoy play as well. One naturalist describes eight wolves playing on an ice pond. The wolves chased each other and skidded on the ice and barked excitedly when one of them would take an out-of-control tumble. He said the wolves reminded him of children at recess.*

> *Did you know that wolf pups, when born, can't see or hear and weigh about one pound?*

(In Praise of Wolves by R.D. Lawrence).

A Wolf is called a PREDATOR because it hunts and feeds on other animals. The animals it hunts are called PREY.

- Wolves that are part of a pack mainly hunt large animals with hooves, called UNGULATES. Moose, elk, deer, mountain sheep, bison and caribou are ungulates. A lone wolf may feed on mice, birds, rabbits, squirrels, beavers, marmots and fish.

- Wolves do not eat three meals a day (with snacks as we do). A wolf may eat only once in four days, and can go as long as two weeks without eating.

- However, the wolf is built in such a way that it makes the "most" of a meal. For example, the simple stomach of an adult wolf can hold as much as fifteen to twenty pounds of meat at one time. That is, a wolf could eat about eighty hamburgers at one meal! The food in a wolf's stomach is digested very quickly. At a kill wolves may feed until "stuffed," rest for a few hours, and then return to eat some more. Because of their meat diet, wolves must drink lots of water.

- Humans often find predator/prey relationships upsetting. But people are predators too. Although most of us do not kill our own food anymore, in the United States over 100,000 cows are made into hamburgers and steaks daily, and more than twelve million chickens are eaten *every day!*

- In the past people believed that wolves and other predators were "bad" animals and that their prey such as deer and elk were "good" animals. But wolves and their prey have lived together for a long time.

- Prey species have developed ways to defend themselves. Their speed and size are great advantages. They also have sharp hooves and in many cases, antlers. A bull moose can weigh 1,250 pounds (an adult wolf weighs only 95 to 100 pounds). A moose is a powerful and dangerous animal to hunt. Wolves are sometimes injured by their prey.

- Usually, wolves kill the young, old, injured and sick. This keeps the prey species healthy by cutting down on the spread of disease and by leaving more food for the stronger animals. It is also good for the individual animal because the wolf often ends the suffering of the sick or injured.

- Scientists studying wolf packs in an area where wolves hunt moose discovered that out of sixteen moose they chased, the wolves were able to bring down only one.

Play "Moose Hunt" on the next page and discover how tough it is to be a predator.

You find an old, sick moose. Take a moose card. Ahead 1 space.

The moose runs towards you, instead of away. Forget it! Back 1 space.

MOOS

DIRECTION

1. You are adult wolves. Hungry pup wait at the den.

2. If you make it back to the den first—with a moose—you win!

3. If you make it back first with *no* moose, you must go around the board again.

4. Cut out the number and moose cards on the corner of the page.

You trespass on another pack's territory. Backtrack before you are discovered.

DEN

PLACE CARDS HERE

START

You lose the trail of your prey. Move back 1 space.

The moose "sensed" you first and got away. Back to Start.

our of your
ibs are broken
y a moose.
Ouch! Back 4
paces.

Mother moose
defends her
calf. Back 1
space.

You and your pack bring
down a moose. You
feast. Take a moose card.
Ahead 1 space.

HUNT

(PLAYERS)

Place number cards in a
k or envelope and take
ns drawing a number
d moving that many spaces.

When you land on a
ce that says you're
uccessful hunter,
e a moose card.

For tokens, use
o origami
lves or two
ferent coins.

Happy
nting!

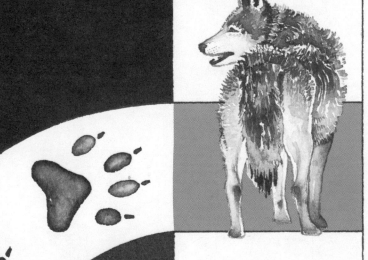

The moose stands its
ground. Back 1 space.

You
find a moose
bogged down in
snow.
Take a
moose
card, and
the short
cut.

In a struggle with a
moose you are gored by
an antler. Back 3 spaces.

1
2
3
4

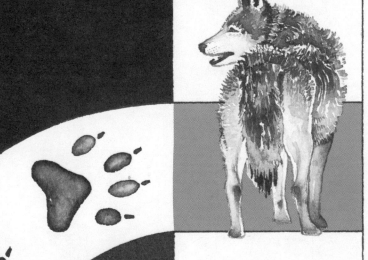

Cut along dotted lines to make cards.

Connect the dots and discover the creature with whom the wolf shares a special relationship.

■ Hints: This animal often follows the wolf to his kill and then "helps himself" after the wolf has eaten. This animal has been observed in the wild playing a kind of "tag" with the wolf. Like the wolf, the "Mystery Animal" is very social.

Can you run as fast as a wolf? Wolves have been timed running 25 to 40 mph. (An average person can run about 6 to 9 mph.)

V   R   N   E   A

_ _   _ _   _ _   _ _   _ _

■ Hint: Unscramble these letters

WOLF WORD PUZZLE

● **DOWN CLUES**

1. When a wolf wants to play, he tells another by this facial expression, a play _____.
2. A wolf hunts its _____.
3. The position a wolf assumes to communicate that he wants to play!
4. By urinating on rocks, trees, etc. the wolf is scent-_____ his territory.
6. The wolf _____ is an important part of the West Coast People's ritual, Kloo-kwalah.
8. Animals that are on the verge of extinction are _____.
10. A wolf that leaves the pack in search of a mate is called a _____.
11. The area in which an animal lives, its home.
16. This bird shares a special relationship with the wolf.
17. A young wolf.

● **ACROSS CLUES**

5. To share feelings and information.
7. Usually five to eight wolves make up a wolf_____.
8. If no animals of a particular species are alive, that species is_____.
9. The leader of the wolf pack is the _____ animal.
12. Where wolf pups are born and raised.
13. Animals with hoofs are called _____. They are the main food of the wolf pack.
14. Animals that are plentiful in some parts of the world but are being reduced in numbers are _____.
15. The area in which a wolf pack lives and hunts.
17. An animal that hunts other species for food.

● **WORD LIST:**

ALPHA
BOW
COMMUNICATE
DEN
ENDANGERED
EXTINCT
GRIN
HABITAT
LONER
MARKING
MASK
PACK
PREDATOR
PREY
PUP
RAVEN
TERRITORY
THREATENED
UNGULATES

Answers on page 52.

Habitat hidden animals are:
3 mice, 2 marmots, 2 beaver, 1 rabbit, 1 deer, 2 elk, 1 moose.

Mystery animal:
raven

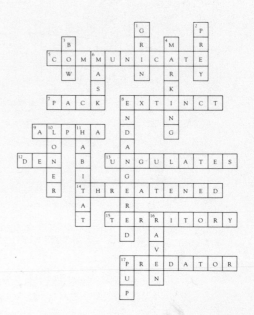

BIBLIOGRAPHY

Arima, E.Y. 1983. *The West Coast (Nootka) People.* British Columbia, Provincial Museum, Victoria, B.C.

Atkinson-Berg, Karlyn. 1983. *Wolves and Humans; Teachers Materials.* The Science Museum of Minnesota, St. Paul, Minnesota,

Brandenburg, Jim. 1988. *White Wolf: Living With An Arctic Legend.* Northword Press, Inc., Minocqua, Wisconsin.

Drucker, Philip. 1951. *The Northern and Central Nootkan Tribes.* Government Printing Office, Smithsonian Institution, Washington, D.C.

Harrington, Fred, H. and Paul C. Paquet. 1982. *Wolves of the World.* Noyes Publications, Park Ridge, New Jersey.

Johnson, Sylvia, A. and Alice Aamodt. 1985. *Wolf Pack, Tracking Wolves in the Wild.* Lerner Publications Company, Minneapolis, Minnesota.*

Lawrence, R.D. 1986. *In Praise of Wolves.* Henry Holt and Company, New York.

_____. 1980. *Secret Go the Wolves,* Ballentine Books, New York.

Lopez, Barry Holstun. 1978. *Of Wolves and Men.* Charles Scribner's Sons, New York.

McLoughlin, John C. 1983. *The Canine Clan: A New Look at Man's Best Friend.* The Viking Press, New York.

Mech, L. David. 1988. *The Arctic Wolf: Living With the Pack.* Voyageur Press, Inc., Stillwater, Minnesota.

_____. 1970. *The Wolf: The Ecology and Behavior of an Endangered Species.* The Natural History Press, Garden City, New York.

Sendey, John. 1977. *The Nootkan Indian: A Pictorial.* Alberni Valley Museum, Port Alberni, B.C., Canada.

Tilt, Whitney and Ruth Norris and Amos Eno. 1987. *Wolf Recovery in the Northern Rocky Mountains.* National Audubon Society and National Fish and Wildlife Foundation, Washington, D.C.

Wexo, John Bonnett. 1986. *Wolves: Zoobooks 2.* Wildlife Education, Ltd., San Diego, California.*

Teton Science School. 1987. *Looking at the Wolf.* Roberts Rinehart Publishers, Inc., Boulder, Colorado.

_____. 1980. *The Indian Book.* World Book—Childcraft International, Inc., Chicago, Illinois.*

Books of interest to younger readers.